THE LITTLE BOOK
OF CATS

THE LITTLE BOOK OF CATS

Brigitte Bulard-Cordeau

CONTENTS

A myriad of cats	8
The origins	12
The species	14
Domestication	16
The sacred cat of Egypt	18
The legends of Asia	20
The legends of Europe	22
The cat in the middle-ages	24
The cat and the witches	26
Popular beliefs	28
Proverbs	30
The cats and the fairies	32
The cat, the woman and the moon	34
Cats of the famous	36
Ailurophobes	38
Famous cats	40
Cats in poetry	42
French literature	44
Foreign literature	46
Writers and cats	48
Tales	50
Puss in Boots	52
Cats in song	54
Nursery rhymes	56
Cats in painting	58
The sculpture	60

IN THE MOVIES	62
THE INSPIRATOR OF MUSICIANS	64
THE CAT AND MUSIC	66
THE ANIMATED CAT	68
ADVERTISEMENT	70
A MINIATURE FELINE	72
A PREDATOR	74
FUR	76
THE CAT AND THE WOMAN	78
THE CAT AND THE CHILD	80
THE MATERNAL INSTINCT	82
BETWEEN CATS AND DOGS	84
CAT EYES	86
THE GAZE	88
NIGHT VISION	90
THE MASTER OF THE HOUSEHOLD	92
BODY LANGUAGE	94
VERBAL LANGUAGE	96
MEOWING	98
PURRING	100
SLEEP	102
GROOMING	104
THE ORDINARY SENSES	106
THE SIXTH SENSE	108
THE GROOMING OF THE KITTEN	110
THE FIRST DAYS	112
THE FIRST GAMES	114
LEARNING HUNTING	116
THE FIGHTS	118

The socialization of the kitten	120
Cat dialogue	122
Outdoor life	124
Indoor life	126
At home	128
A delicate palate	130
The cat and the plants	132
Solitude	134
The purebred	136
The competition cat	138
Silhouette	140
The coat	142
The range of breeds	144
History of breeds	146
Exotic cats	148
The persian	150
The siamese	152
The angora	154
The chartreux	156
The sacred cat of Burma	158
The European	160
The Norwegian	162
The maine coon	164
Caring for cats	166
The cat of the 21ST century	168
Bibliography ans sources of quotations	170

A MYRIAD OF CATS

Portraits of cats
The cat inspires all artists: sculptors, painters, photographers and filmmakers have painted with curiosity the portrait of this elegant animal, funny and always changing. This was the case with Jean-Jacques Bachelier, Théophile-Alexandre Steinlein, Maurice Denis, Picasso, Leonor Fini … who immortalized the feline gbreed that the writer Celine associated with witchcraft. The body of the cat is a parade of images, varying according to the positions and the mimics that it adopts. The little feline rests in a ball, in a crescent, taking the attitude of a sphinx, as if it had been sculpted, or else the belly in the air, symbolizing absolute peace. All of these attitudes reflect the utmost confidence in his surroundings. It is also seen to surrender totally to the arms of Morpheus or, seated with the body in a C-shape and legs in V-shape, lick's itself belly to groom itself, when suddenly sees some wave or movement. Its ears, urged by a noise imperceptible to us, turn then like weathervanes. Is it an invisible gnat, a dust that a ray of sun illuminates? Whatever it is, the cat returns suddenly to its predatory nature. It crouches, jumps, twirls, catches, taps, knocks and gives the final blow to the victim. And it does not matter whether this one is real or imaginary!

"A tiger to caress"

The cat becomes a lion, leopard or meerkat, when he stands on its hind legs to watch the surroundings. It thus knows how to satisfy the fantasies of those who, every day, have the "pleasure of having a tiger to caress," to quote Joseph Méry in La Comédie des animaux (1862). The cat, with its slender silhouette and its movement, takes on various and incongruous forms. It also moves from concentration to reactivity when it hunts, from contemplation to meditation when it observes people and the landscape, yet never leaves its secret universe nor departs from its sense of mystery. The cat is always between two worlds, the real and the unreal. Was it not, for all these reasons, raised to the rank of god by the Egyptians in antiquity?

"His eyes shine like diamonds"

The discovery in 2004 in Cyprus of a burial house for a man and his cat suggests that the domestication of the cat is on this island. It would date back 10,000 years! The main asset of the cat at that time? Its talent as a hunter, which allows men to get rid of rodents, vectors of epidemics. The cat then penetrates little by little into the houses, where it shares the lives of men. We take pleasure in caressing its soft fur, and it lets himself be taken in the arms by the children. Its domestication, however, passes through extreme phases, and its integration is far from final. Thus, in medieval Europe, the cat is hated and burnt. It is suspected of being a supporter of Satan and a friend of witches. An image of the cat very different from ours haunts the spirits: that of an animal with sharp claws, mad eyes and bristly hairs. The black cat in particular has no gbreed in the eyes of men. After being demonized, the cat finds its place as a pet and it is rehabilitated."Do not doubt it, in societies, at shows, promenades, balls, even in academies, cats will be received, or rather sought after," wrote François-Augustin de Paradis de Moncrif at the beginning of the eighteenth century. He was ridiculed for this. Yet he was a visionary. For the cat is studied shortly afterwards by scientists, such as the naturalist Buffon, in his Natural History. And many literary figures, such as Charles Perrault, Victor Hugo, Baudelaire, Edgar Poe, Théophile Gautier, Maupassant and Colette, later left literary portraits of cats that captivated their contemporaries.

Good as Gold
Colors and strokes of pencil in some, atmosphere and mystery in others ... illustrators created the image of a flirtatious cat, naughty, charming and affectionate. It became a key figure in the advertising center, serving as a spokesperson for products as different as Meunier Chocolate or Hoffmann Starch, as seen in the pictures of this book. Represented as tame in the midst of pretty ladies, or an intrepid player when the accomplice of children who play, or just tender and protective, the cat attracts sympathy, and its timeless charm, whatever the setting of these illustrations, is always effective.

The image of the cat in the 21st century

Today it is presented as the animal of the 21st century. Its population exceeds that of the dog in France. There are 10.7 million small cats (with a growth of 6.5% between 2006 and 2008) against 7.8 million dogs. The cat is considered by the ethologists as an animal very close to man, which was hoped in the eighteenth century by Francis Augustin de Paradis de Moncrif: "It is impossible that one should not feel that in one's Cat, one possesses a friend of very good company, an admirable pantomime, a born astrologer, a perfect musician, and finally an assemblage of talents and gbreeds; But we cannot yet determine precisely when this century will be so legitimately compared with the golden age." This golden age, so desired by this court writer, will be the one that presents an image of the cat that is more reasoned and true. May this work give us "cat eyes," to see the cat without blinders, as a precious friend.

THE ORIGINS

It is at home everywhere, able to enter everywhere, the animal that passes silently, the silent prowler.
GUY DE MAUPASSANT

The cat belongs to the Felidae family, which dates back to the Oligocene - between 34 and 25 million years ago. There are at this time two subfamilies: the nimravidae, the size of a lynx to that of a panther, and the felines, the size of a cat. The smilodon is probably the first feline that Man met. Its reign lasted for a long time, since it existed at the time of the Miocene, 23 million years ago. This ancestor of the cats lived in America. It had the appearance of a tiger - short tail and stocky limbs - and has canines 20 centimeters in length in the form of saber. A specimen of this animal found in the Rancho La Brea Pit (United States) and dating back 1 million years is exhibited at the National Museum of Natural History in Paris. In this museum is also shown a skeleton of eusmilus. From the size of a puma, this primitive feline dating back to 34 million years had the slow gait but a quick bite. All these ancestors of the present cat originated in Asia during the Pleiocentocene - between 3 and 1 million years ago, where they developed in the steppes and savannah-rich game, before dispersing all over the world.

THE SPECIES

Only vulgar nature disregard the distinguished character of this animal.

CHAMPFLEURY

The domestic cat was long considered to be descended from the only wild cat, *Felis silvestris*. Indeed, attracted by easy food, it would gradually have become domesticated by man until it became a familiar animal. Its first places of domestication were reportedly located in Libya, the domain of *Felis silvestris libyca*, and in Pakistan, home of the *Felis silvestris ornata*, where it still lives in the wild. Today, researchers believe that there are three species of wildcats found on three continents: - the European wild cat, *Felis silvestris silvestris* tris (called "forest cat"), has spread In a vast area encompassing all of continental Europe and extending to the eastern borders of Turkey; - the Asian wild cat *Felis silvestris ornataornata* (known as the "ornate cat") lives in South-West Asia, Iran, Pakistan and India; - the wild cat of Africa, or Libyan wild cat, *Felis silvestris libyca* (called "gloved cat"), evolves from an area ranging from North Africa to the Arabian Peninsula.

D'abord moi! je n'aime pas les bruns

DOMESTICATION

The cat wave makes that one is feline or not feline, that one is born F or not F.
FERNAND MÉRY

The dog was the first animal domesticated by man, when we were still nomadic hunters. The cat was domesticated only at the time of the first sedentary populations who practiced agriculture. Appreciated for its talent as a hunter, the feline was indeed little by little invited to stay in the houses to track rodents, until it became a pet. It has long been thought that this domestication dates from the Neolithic period (9000-3300 BC). But the discovery of a burial containing a man and a cat in the village of Shillourokambos, Cyprus, pushed back even further the date of the taming of the cat. The animal could indeed been man's friend for more than 10,000 years! This discovery made in 2004 is perhaps the proof that the island was the native land of the domestic cat, before Egypt.

LES CHATS

THE SACRED CAT OF EGYPT

*In thought, they take on the noble attitudes of
the great sphinxes lying in the depths of solitudes.*
CHARLES BAUDELAIRE

Considered a god in Egypt, the cat is the companion of kings and high dignitaries. From the eleventh dynasty (2134-1991 BC), he was the favorite of the Theban king Montuhotep II. Other great figures in Egyptian history cherished him: Queen Tiyi, wife of Amenophis III (1408-1372 BC) and the elder brother of King Amenophis IV (1372-1354 BC). Prince Tuthmosis, for example. During the twelfth dynasty (1991-1785 BC), the Egyptians raised sacred cats in the temple of Amon, in Heliopolis. The famous *Book of the Dead of the ancient Egyptians* mentions the great cat that lives in this city, beside Ra, the sun god. Later, the popularity of the cat increased during the reign of Amenophis IV. The Egyptians then regarded him as a representation of the divine. The cat will even enter the Egyptian pantheon in the form of Bastet. This goddess, with the body of a woman and the head of a cat, symbolizing love and procreation, was venerated in Bubastis and Saqqarah, where a temple, the Bubasteion, was dedicated to her. But the veneration which the Egyptians professed for this animal does not stop there: they mummified it in the same way as they did men!

THE LEGENDS OF ASIA

And I salute in you, calm thinker, two exquisite virtues: skepticism and sweetness.
JULES LEMAÎTRE

In Asia, the cat has a very positive image. It is considered a protective animal, almost like a talisman. It is even attributed extrasensory gifts. In Japan, for example, sailors believe in the power of the mike-neko, the tricolor cat, white, red and black, which, by climbing the mast of ships, takes away the souls of shipwrecked navigators. An Asian legend proclaims the philosophy of the cat. Indeed, of all the animals gathered around the body of Buddha to mourn his death, the cat and the serpent were the only ones to believe in the immortality of the wise man. Another legend, from Indochina, explains the origin of the sacred Burmese cat. It is said that a white cat called Sinh, whose "ears, tail, nose and extremity of the limbs were of the color of the ground," remained beside the sapphire-goddess Tsun Kyan Tse. One day, when the high priest Mun Ha came to die, and his soul had to penetrate the body of an animal, it was Sinh who was chosen. The cat's eyes then became "blue, immense and deep as the eyes of the goddess." That is why, from that day, it was forbidden to kill a cat under penalty of being "condemned to suffer your whole life."

THE LEGENDS OF EUROPE

When I play with my kitty, who knows if she enjoys her time with me more than I do with her?
MICHEL DE MONTAIGNE

Legend has it that the manx, a cat living on the Isle of Man, between Great Britain and Ireland, had its tail cut off when it embarked on Noah's Ark. Noah would have closed the door of the boat as the cat entered. The Flood inspired other legends about the cat, supposedly born of an enormous sneeze of the lion that was on the ark. Russian literature is full of stories that present a malicious and very cunning cat. A Polish legend sheds light on the birth of the kittens that bloom in spring on the trees. It says that willows, hearing a cat weep as she had been thrown into the river, stretched out their long branches to serve as moorings for its little ones and saved them. Since then, every May, the willows bear velvety leaves like the hair of the kittens.

THE CAT IN THE MIDDLE AGES

Friends of science and voluptuousness, they seek the silence and the horror of darkness.
CHARLES BAUDELAIRE

The cat did not have the same destiny in Europe in the Middle Ages as in ancient Egypt. In medieval times, it is indeed linked with the devil and is accused of being the companion of witches. At the end of the eleventh century, Catholics referred to the followers of dualistic heresy as "cathares," meaning "pure" in Greek, but more readily associated with the Latin word catus, the "cat," to accuse them of being Satan's servants. At that time, there were also massacres of cats. Hated and vilified, they were tortured and then burned during festivals which consisted, on the day of the summer solstice, of throwing cats from the top of a tower in the midst of a joyful crowd. Some cities have also carved a solid reputation as ailurophobes (those who hate cats). This tradition of massacre did not end until 1733 in Metz and in 1817 in Ypres. In Scotland too, until the seventeenth century, there was a barbaric ceremony, the *taghairm* (devil's supper), during which, for two days, cats were impaled and then roasted.

THE CAT AND THE WITCHES

And I am your friend, for no creature has understood my sober strangeness better than you.
MAURICE ROLLINAT

It is in the narratives of the trials of witchcraft that the incontestable link between the cat and the witches appears best. Most of the time, it is a black cat, associated with the image of Satan. Thus, in 1556, Anna Winkelzipfel, a very famous witch from Bergheim in Alsace, was burned for having entered, covered in black cat skins, the room of a certain Jacques Potter. The old women of Obernai, another village in Alsace, used to transform themselves into black cats to sneak into the stables, where they harmed the cattle. The sorceress Jeanne Boille was executed in Vesoul in 1620 for having been in contact with a demon who appeared to her in the form of a monstrous black cat. There are also woodcuts from the seventeenth century which represent witches going out on the Sabbath, accompanied by cats. People believed that these animals possessed the power to fly on a broom to join decadent festivals. Whatever the color of the cats, their fate was the same as that of the witches, namely, to be burnt alive on a pyre in the midst of a joyous crowd.

POPULAR BELIEFS

*When the mice eat the cats,
the king will be Lord of Arras.*
PROVERB

The mysteries surrounding the cat have engendered many popular beliefs and superstitions. At the beginning of the twentieth century, Paul Sébillot, in *Le Folklore de France* (1904-1906), gathered an impressive number of sayings, traditions and fables related to the animal world. The cat is a star character, regardless of the region of France. In the Vosges, to cross a cat on New Year's day meant three hundred and sixty-five days of misfortune. Among the Normans, seeing a cat on its way when one had to deal with business meant you had to turn back immediately. A whole day is cursed in Provence when you saw kittens playing in the morning. In Brittany, it was necessary to take care not to confide a secret in the presence of a cat, even if it were asleep, for it would be revealed. Among the Angevins, it was feared that a cat would enter a bakery while the dough was poured into the baskets, for this would mean that the dough could not rise or that the bread would be burnt. Lastly, beware of cats born in the month of the Virgin, as *the Gospel of the Cattails* indicates, a unique book on beliefs dating from the fifteenth century, for it is said that "nothing was as bad as a May cat!"

PROVERBS

Do not wake the sleeping cat.
PROVERB

Cats were born to chase rats and catch them, the proverb says. The association of cats with rats is common: there are many old French expressions and puns that play on the word for cat, "chat." In "To good cat, good rat," the saying means that a good offense requires a good defense. Even better known is the proverb that inspired many illustrators: "When the cat's away, the mice will play." It alludes to the fact that in the boss's absence, all falls into chaos and hilarity. Note that this proverb also exists in Creole, and is common in Yemen. In popular wisdom, the cat is not only a hunter, but is also related to the idea of beauty: expressions in several languages use the image of the cat to say that charm and attraction are more powerful than beauty. Moreover, the character of the cat is often present in the sayings that deal with trade: "Do not buy with a cat in pocket" means that it is necessary to examine a matter carefully before making a deal. And finally, "There's no such thing as a kitten that doesn't scratch" advises caution in recalling that there is no harmless enemy, no matter how small.

4° On est puni par où l'on a péché!

THE CAT AND THE FAIRIES

Mirou spoke in the language of the gods and in almanac verse.
Jean Lorrain

The mysteries of the cat, as well as its resourcefulness, have propelled it into the world of fantastic and enchanting characters. The friend of the witches with the disastrous practices frequents the fairy Carabosse, but this one isn't a good fairy and brings only misfortune in creating havoc in the destiny of men. In the tales of the Grimm brothers, the cat also has more often the face of a frightening old witch than that of a magical fairy magician. Thus, in the story Jorinde and Joringel, the Queen of the witches takes on the appearance of a cat or an owl. But the cat is not always a bird of woe! Intelligent and sophisticated, even philosophical, it's also a genius with good intentions. The cat in *Good Little Henri* does not skimp on the right words to persuade Henri to set out on a dangerous journey, which according to the good fairy will allow him to regain his health.

THE CAT, THE WOMAN AND THE MOON

I never understood that meat did not belong to cats.
MAURICE GENEVOIX

In ancient Egypt, Bastet, a cat-headed woman, is the lunar goddess. Plutarch, the Greek author of the first century, writes in his *works on Isis and Osiris* on the reason for the association between this goddess and the moon. According to him, it has to do with gestation of the cat. In ancient times, it was believed that this animal could be pregnant seven times in its life and bear twenty-eight kittens, figures that refer to the menstrual cycle of the woman and the number of days in the lunar month. The link established between the woman, the moon and the cat also found an echo in art, especially in architecture. Heads of cats, as round as the moon, appear on certain monuments. The portal of the Saint-Michel Church in Lescure near Albi, a masterpiece of Benedictine Romanesque art (1150), is a fine example of this. It features a frieze with twenty-four heads of cats, representing the hours in a day.

CATS OF THE FAMOUS

He sometimes regretted not being a cat and getting to spend his life in such good company.
MADAME D'AULNOY

Throughout history, the cat has been adored by the great men and women of the world. At the time of Louis XIV and Louis XV, the women of the court delighted in the company of cats: Marie Leszczynska, wife of Louis XV, Duchess of Maine, wife of one of Louis XIV's sons, Duchess of Montespan, Princess Palatine, wife of the Duke of Orleans, and the Marchioness of Deffaud, never ceased to praise Her Majesty the Cat. Cardinal de Richelieu, whose favorite cat was named Lucifer, also owned several of them, which he endowed with fanciful names. The cat was the ally of other illustrious politicians: Clemenceau, Poincare, Churchill, who bequeathed a part of his fortune to his cat Jock, and General de Gaulle also loved feline company. Certain American Presidents shared this fondness too: Abraham Lincoln adopted three starving cats, Theodore Roosevelt never organized a gala in the White House without his cat Slippers present, John F. Kennedy liked them, and Bill Clinton was shy to show his cat Socks to members of the press!

AILUROPHOBES

Good cat, good rat.
PROVERB

Cats were not loved by all historical figures. Many illustrious leaders, from Julius Caesar to Napoleon, passing through Ambrose Pare, Charles IX and Henry II, detested cats. Among the ailurophobes (people who hate cats), there were also Pope Gregory IX, King Louis XII, writers La Fontaine and Voltaire, and scientist Georges Cuvier. Even in the eighteenth century, when cats enjoyed a strong current of appreciation, Buffon (1707-1788) knocks on the the animal in his book *Natural History*, where he writes: "The cat is an infidel servant that must be kept only by necessity, to oppose it to another domestic enemy, even more inconvenient, and which cannot be driven out." This famous French naturalist considered the cat to be a "determined thief." He even accuses it of "innate malice" and endows it with a "false character, a perverse character, which with age is still increasing, and which training only masks." However, the life of some authors sometimes contradicts their writings: Ronsard proclaimed his phobia of cats, but welcomed them under his roof; Maupassant confesses his hatred for this animal while taking pleasure in caressing it.

FAMOUS CATS

I love that cats have this independent character and are almost ungrateful, never attaching themselves to anyone.

FRANÇOIS-RENÉ DE CHATEAUBRIAND

Today we remember many famous cat's names. Meneghetto was the cat of the Venetian painter Jacopo Bassano (1510-1592), who never ceased to praise him. At the same time, Belaud lived in France. The poet Du Bellay (1522-1560) devoted an ode to him. Cardinal de Richelieu (1585-1642), for his part, owned a series of cats which he particularly liked and to which he had attributed the most fantastic names: Pyrame, Thisbe, Gazette, Soumise, Wig, Racan, Felimare, Serpolet and Lucifer. There was also Micetto, the cat of Pope Leo XII, who went to Chateaubriand (1768-1848) as an inheritance. "The Pope's little cat has just been brought to me: he is all gray and very gentle like his former master," wrote the great romantic writer to Madame Recamier in 1829. It is also impossible to forget Saha, Colette's cat (1873-1954), as well as Moumoune blanche and Moumoutte chinoise, Pierre Loti's two cats (1850-1923), who became the main characters in her novel. More recently, Philippe Ragueneau (1917-2003) made his cat, Moune, the hero of a series of novels.

CATS IN POETRY

Cats, mysterious and delicate, no longer obedient even to the good God, who smiles [...].
FRANCIS JAMMES

Poetry shines a spotlight on the cat, whose elegance and gbreed are perfectly suited to the delights of writing. In 1558, Joachim Du Bellay devoted an ode to his Chartreux cat named Belaud: "A small leonine muzzle / Around which was planted / A silvery barbelette, / Armed with a small follet hair / His damoiselet musequin. Three hundred years later, Charles Baudelaire, in *Les Fleurs du mal* (1861), dedicated several poems to the cat. The poet describes the fur, elastic body and voice which "contains all the ecstasies." He also evokes his gaze in the *Petits Poèmes en prose* (1861-1862), and assures that in it he sees eternity. Many of the poems devoted to the cat are in a lively style, like that of the *Little Cat* (in *Les Musardises*, 1911) by Edmond Rostand: "It is a little black cat, cheeky as a page." Pablo Neruda also praises this animal in his *Ode to the Cat* (1959), and Paul Eluard writes this magnificent verse in The Animals and *Their Men, the Men and Their Animals* (1920): "When the Cat Dances / It's to isolate his prison / And when he thinks / It is up to wall of his eyes."

FRENCH LITERATURE

The only risk in spending time with a cat is that of enrichment.
Colette

The cat has inspired writers and poets of all time. But it was towards the middle of the seventeenth century that it made its entry into French literature. At the time Cardinal Richelieu showed his adoration for the cat by adopting several, and it became clear that the friendship between the cat and its master was possible. Jean de La Fontaine (1621-1695) included it many times in his *Fables*. In the eighteenth century, François-Augustin of Paradis de Moncrif (1687-1770) rehabilitated the animal, martyred in the Middle Ages, and published a *History of cats*. In the nineteenth century, Champfleury (1821-1889) had a great literary success with *Les Chats* (1869), illustrated by drawings by Delacroix, Viollet-le-Duc and Mérimée. Interest in this animal increased until the twentieth century. In *Le Chat de Babaud Monnier*, Jean Lorrain (1855-1906) describes a cat who "had the gift of speech, just like a man". At the same time, Pierre Loti (1850-1923) signed *Lives of Two Cats*, and Colette (1873-1954), author of *La Chatte, Mitsou, La Paix chez les bêtes*..., became the most expert writer in feline psychology. Today, stories about cats, such as Philippe Ragueneau's *Les Aventures du Cat Moune* (1983), have gained a new audience.

FOREIGN LITERATURE

*A learned cat is more curious [...]
than a young boy whose stories have been stuffed
with incoherent things.*
ERNST THEODOR AMADEUS HOFFMANN

Lazy but cunning in Spanish literature, attracting popular sympathy among Italian authors, fantastic in Anglo-Saxon literature, philosophical among German writers... The cat shows a different face from one sort of foreign literature to another. It is a scholarly cat described by the German author of the early nineteenth century Ernst Theodor Amadeus Hoffmann in *The Life and Opinions of the Tomcat Murr* (1819 and 1821), whose head is "wide enough to contain all the sciences." At the same time, American literature carried the start of an interest in the cat, which is found in Edgar Poe's story *The Black Cat* (1843). It is Baudelaire who translates it and publishes it in *The New Extraordinary Stories* in 1857. In his translation, he perfectly tells of the curse that touches the cat Pluto, persecuted by his master. There is more gaiety and humor in Italian literature. Fabio Tombari, in *The Book of Animals* (1956), tells the story of Marette's life, who, as a little black kitten "too fat, a little stupid and a little foolish, was nicknamed first "Napoleon". Then, as he hardly stirred from his chair, he was renamed "Mister Placid"."

WRITERS AND CATS

The inkwell never runs out when it comes to writing about cats.
JEAN-LOUIS HUE

The cat is the ideal companion to awaken man's imagination. They become muses. Its silence respects that of the writer and its communicative well-being is conducive to the writer's literary exploration. A perfect osmosis can thus prevail between a writer and his cat. So much so that Theophile Gautier wrote in *Portraits and Literary Souvenirs* (1875): "It seems that the cats guess the idea that descends from the brain to the tip of the pen, and that, stretching their paw, they would like to seize it in passing." Most authors who owned a cat gave a vibrant tribute to their companion. Jean Lorrain, for example, expresses his feline fable in *Le Chat de Babaud Monnier*, published in 1903. The writers and poets Chateaubriand, Victor Hugo, Theophile Gautier, Honoré de Balzac, Alexandre Dumas, Charles Baudelaire, Émile Zola, François Coppée, Pierre Loti, Stéphane Mallarmé, Paul Léautaud, Jean Giraudoux and Colette are also among the illustrious fans of the little feline.

TALES

Or become a girl, or make me a cat!
MADAME D'AULNOY

In 1697, Charles Perrault's *Tales of Mother L'Oye* were published. The cat is the star of the work, as Puss in Boots. Its story bears a moral, which shows that "Industry and know-how / are better than acquired goods. In the same year, Madame d'Aulnoy published The White Cat, with other tales that also appeal to children today. In 1885, it was Lewis Carroll's turn to imagine the Cheshire Cat, an important figure of *Alice in Wonderland*. It appears and disappears at will, in whole or in part; Which makes Alice say: "I have already seen a cat without a smile, but a smile without a cat..." Ten years later, Loys Brueyre's "*Les Contes populaires de la Bretagne*" is about an orphan, Dick Whittington, whose destiny changes thanks to his cat Gib. Author of fantastic tales, Guy de Maupassant also makes a cat into a hero in *Misti, Memories of a Boy* (1884). He maintains that jealousy is a feline feeling. Indeed, the witch says that her cat Mouton once jumped in the face of her lover, tearing her skin with claws, "as if it were a cloth of linen." The art of the tale is to make us believe in the worst...

PUSS IN BOOTS

Do not grieve my master; you have only to give me a bag and make me make a pair of boots.
CHARLES PERRAULT

In 1697, Charles Perrault published *Tales of Mother L'Oye*. In *Puss in Boots*, the animal, dressed in large boots and endowed with a bag, is full of imagination. Among his adventures, this very smart cat outwits an ogre.
—"I have been assured," said the cat, "that you had the gift of changing you in all sorts of animals; that you could, for example, transform yourself into a lion, an elephant."
—"That is true," replied the ogre suddenly, "and to show it to you, you are going to see me become a lion."
—"I have also been assured," said the cat, "but I cannot believe it; that you have the power to take the form of the smallest animals: for example, to transform into a rat, into a mouse…"
The ogre runs, turns into a mouse, and is immediately crunched by the cat. Puss in Boots is also able to save his master from misery. He invented for him the title of Marquis de Carabas. It is the way to attract the king's attention and dazzle him! In each of his tales, Charles Perrault included moral. In *Puss in Boots*, he emphasizes how resourcefulness, imagination and the will to recover from unfavorable situations are values far superior to riches acquired.

CATS IN SONG

Cat, cat, cat, [...]
Do not you hear the mice dancing
in entrechat on the floor??
Tristan Klingsor

Songwriters, comedians, poets and musical groups are happy to include reference to cats. Its single syllable has a pleasant sound and allows them to juggle with words. If the result is indeed melodious, it doesn't always make sense. Jean Constantin, in the 1950^s, enthuses in his song *Le Pacha*: "It was a cat / pacha / Persian cat." The main thing here in the wording is the pleasant rebound! In song, the character of the cat can have an almost philosophical scope: "They grow old in small cat steps / The bigots, the bigots," sings Jacques Brel in *Les Bigotes* (1962). Cats also appear as the constant companion and witness to events. The cat is particularly present when it comes to comforting the elderly during a bereavement. This is the theme developed in Cats, a comedy by Andrew Llyod Webber, played for the first time in London in 1981. Today, many singers still bring up the cat, such as the Pow Wow group, which sings '*I wanna be a cat*,' and singer Nolwenn, who for one of her albums used the Cheshire Cat, from *Alice in Wonderland*.

NURSERY RHYMES

Cats are very advantageously organized for music.
FRANÇOIS-AUGUSTIN DE PARADIS DE MONCRIF

The word "cat," with its short, light sound, can be sung easily and cheerfully. This is why this monosyllabic word, which has inspired the minstrels of all ages, often serves as a basis for the composition of children's songs. It's a word we repeat and rhyme. Used in a playful way, it allows poetic licenses and inventions, and comes back as a leitmotiv: "Three little cats, three little cats, three little cats, cats, cats." In the nursery rhyme, the role of the cat is to stimulate the sensitivity of toddlers while amusing them. In *It's Mother Michel*, they imagine the deep desolation of the poor woman " ... who lost her cat, who screams out the window to whomever will bring it back." In another traditional nursery rhyme, the children laugh and then cry when the kitten, who had been clever enough to put the chin rather than the paw in the cheese, is killed by his master. In this same rhyme, the refrain, "And ron and ron / Small patapon," also imitates a purr, which denotes in the songwriter a perfect knowledge of the cat and its purr and uses ingeniously to manifest gaiety and sadness.

CATS IN PAINTING

*A perfect being, more beautiful than all,
better proportioned than the lion and the tiger.*
LEONOR FINI

In the Middle Ages, the cat was found in bestiaries, books depicting animals, and then, from the thirteenth century, in religious images, such as *The Holy Family with the Cat*, by Federico Barocci (1532-1612). Later, painters highlighted the skill of the cat, such as Jean-Jacques Bachelier (1724-1806), in *Cat and Butterfly*, Cecilia Beaux (1855-1942), in *Sita and Sarita* (or *Girl with the Cat*), and Maurice Denis (1870-1943), in *Homage to Cézanne*. Other subjects of choice of the artists: the cat and the woman, illustrated by *La Dame au Chat* (or *The Demanding Cat*) by Pierre Bonnard (1867-1947). The friendship between cats and children is depicted in *Three Children and a Cat* by Richard Parkes Bonington (1802-1828), in *The King of the Cats of Balthus* (1908-2001), and in *Sunday afternoon* by Leonor Fini (1908-1996). Sometimes the painter is also represented next to his cat, like Tsuguharu Foujita (1886-1968) in his *Self-portrait* from 1926. Today, the cat is omnipresent in the naive art of Bernard Vercruyce or the animal painting of Eve Oziol, specialized in the representation of felines.

THE SCULPTURE

*It was a living cat like a hermit devotee,
a cat making a Cattemitte, A holy cat man.*
JEAN DE LA FONTAINE

The statuettes of Bastet, the Egyptian goddess with the head of the cat, show the interest that sculptors have had in cats for millennia. Some Gallo-Roman sculpted tombs represent cats held in the arms of children, like the magnificent stele of Laetus (1st century), discovered in Aquitaine. Later, cat sculptures often appeared in sacred art. The animal, for example, is found at the base of the Celtic Cross of Muiredach, at Monasterboice Abbey (tenth century), in Ireland. On one of the marquees of the cloister of the Cathedral of Tarragona, in Spain, there is also a cat carried by rats, which he then kills in the scene of the next marquee. The late-medieval and Renaissance woodcarvers placed the animal near mice, dogs or women. In the nineteenth century, three great sculptors put the animal at the center of their art: Antoine-Louis Barye (1796-1875), Rembrandt Bugatti (1884-1916) and Theophile-Alexandre Steinlen (1859-1923). In the twentieth century, some works of cats become very famous, such as *The Cat of Bronze*, melted by Valsuani for Picasso (1881-1973), or *The Cat* of Alberto Giacometti (1901-1966). Nowadays, the cat sculptures of a Cévé are a must-see.

IN THE MOVIES

His manners were those of a cat who had seen the court and the beautiful world.

HONORÉ DE BALZAC

At the beginning of the twentieth century, the cat burst onto the silver screen with cartoons. It became a hero in the skin of the malicious *Felix the cat*. It was this character who inspired the Walt Disney studios to create *The Three Orphan Kittens* in 1935, then *Tom and Jerry*, as of 1940. In 1970, 325,000 drawings were needed to tell the story of Duchesse and her three rescued kittens by the dashing Thomas O'Malley in *The Aristocats*. But the cat made its real entrance to the cinema in the 1960's, with Vojtech Jasny 's *The Cassandra Cat* (1962), Walt Disney's *The Incredible Journey* (1963), featuring a Siamese cat named Tao, *That Darned Cat!* (1965) by Robert Stevenson. On the screen, the cat has very different roles. In *Le Cat* (1971) by Pierre Granier Deferre, Jean Gabin and Simone Signoret communicate via cat. In *The Godfather* (1972), with Marlon Brando, the cat is the accomplice of the thieves. In *The Cat From Outer Space* (1978), it's an extraterrestrial. More recently, *The Adventures of Milo and Otis* (1988), by Masanori Hata, and *When The Cat's Away* (1996), by Cédric Klapisch, put cats at the center of the action.

THE INSPIRATOR OF MUSICIANS

*Music is a celestial art, it is certain that
our species has the privilege of it.*
HIPPOLYTE TAINE

The connection between cats and music is very old. It dates back to ancient Egypt, where this animal was associated with the sistrum, the percussion instrument that was emblematic of Isis, the goddess of Love. The cat is a kind of musical instrument with the sounds it expresses. This has inspired instruments with more or less success. The "cat organ," for example, was common in Europe until the beginning of the nineteenth century. For its operation, it was necessary that twenty cats, enclosed in a narrow case, have their tail attached to the keyboard! The cat inspired many musicians: Jules Massenet, Edvard Grieg, Erik Satie, Henri Sauguet, who composed the music of *La Chatte* (1927), Diaghilev's ballet, Darius Milhaud, with his piano work *La Muse Ménagère*, Etc. Musicians also considered the animal's voice as being particularly melodious. Rossini, in his Duo of cats, declines a series of miaous repeated in different tones. In Maurice Ravel's *L'Enfant et les sortilèges* (1919-1925), the music is a parody of meowing kittens and cats in heat.

THE CAT AND MUSIC

Why would there not be real relationships between musical instruments and cats?
François-Augustin de Paradis de Moncrif

Sensitive to sounds, the little feline is able to make a hierarchy of its tastes, and manifest these in its own way. In the movement of its ears, from the front to the rear or from the horizontal to the vertical, one can easily guess its feelings with regard to music. Not all instruments please a cat! They have a clear preference for the violin. The cat hates drum beats, the sound of the horn and the clarinet. Not all notes flatter his ear either. The sharper notes are horrible, while the middle of the fourth octave of the violin puts them in ecstasy. The sound of the piano, on the other hand, fascinates them completely. *Cody, the cat* of Henri Sauguet (1901-1989), rolled on the ground as soon as his master began to play. And if it was a work by Debussy, he would jump on the piano, as if to better listen to his favorite music. It is sometimes fun to consider the animal as a composer, as is the case with *La Fugue du Chat* (1729), which is maliciously attributed to Scarlatti's cat. In reality, the animal, which loved to run blithely on the keyboard of the harpsichord, one day inspired his master, who took a score to transpose the notes he heard.

THE ANIMATED CAT

*I scold when I'm happy and
I wag his tail when I'm angry.*
LEWIS CARROLL

Despite the success of the *Tribulations of a cat* by Benjamin Rabier in 1905, it was with *Krazy Kat*, published in 1910, the true adventure of the cat in the comic strip began. In this album by George Herriman, the androgynous cat is in love with Ignatz, the mocking mouse. This character influences in the 1920's the creators of *Felix the cat*, the Americans Otto Messmer and Pat Sullivan. After the creation of *Tom and Jerry* by Joseph Barbera and William Hanna in the 1940^s, other cartoons featured cats: in *Titi* by Chase Craig (1942), the yellow canary is eternally chased by Sylvestre. In the 1950^s José Cabrero Arnal created the cat Hercules, companion to the dog Pif. In 1978's Garfield, Jim Davis' red-haired cat, met with great success thanks to his unforgettable phrases ("I'm lazy, fat and I brag about it.") Ten years later, Disney Studios released *Oliver and Company*, whose hero is a kitten. More recently, other cats have won over the hearts of comic lovers everywhere: *Le Chat* (since 1986) by Philippe Geluck, *Billy The Cat* (since 1990), Colman and Desberg's kitten, and *The Rabbi's Cat* (since 2002) by Joann Sfar.

ADVERTISEMENT

Cats have other ideas than dogs on life.
Octave Mirbeau

Hoffmann starch, Craven cigarettes, Dubonnet wine... The cat has long been an excellent spokesperson to promote brands! It was chosen to attract at first glance consumers' attention on products to buy. Nothing stopped the advertisers from getting to the housewife: they dressed the cat, gave it the role of a pretty lady or made it a scoundrel who did not hesitate to steal the fish from a baby's plate. In the age of television and mass media, the animal became the faithful messenger of some major brands. With its green eyes shining like car headlights, it promotes Goodyear tires. It also highlights the comfort of Ikea furniture. Advertising is constantly using it, not only, of course, for the promotion of a brand of cat food, but also for promoting products that at first sight have nothing to do with cats: Laundry, Hi-Fi, and more.

A MINIATURE FELINE

God made the cat to give man the pleasure of caressing the tiger.
JOSEPH MÉRY

The cat has an athlete's body. Its bones and muscles are identical to those of big cats. The 250 bones of the cat are equipped with modifiable joints, which allows it for example to curve its back to 180 degrees. The vertebral column comprises 50 vertebrae, composed of 7 cervical, 13 thoracic, 7 lumbar, 3 sacral and welded vertebrae and 20 coccygeal. The rib cage is made up of 13 pairs of ribs. It is thanks to this framework that the cat enjoys great agility. It can, for example, move in a straight line along the alleys, like a tightrope walker. Moreover, its musculature is composed of 500 muscles which make its body extensible. The cat can jump very high and land smoothly, as well as stretch long to relax. Its qualities of balance, suppleness and agility are also due to its perfectly coordinated nervous system, its movable tail, which serves as its balance-weight, and its retractile claws.

Felis euptilura
Tigerkatze
Tiger cat
Chat tigré

A PREDATOR

Who does not feed the cat feeds the rat.
PROVERB

The cat combines all the physical and anatomical features of the predator. It's sort of a miniature tiger. It has the same mouth in reduced size as the larger feline cousin. Its lips (its "chops") ensure a maximum opening of the jaws. On the 30 teeth, there are 12 incisors. There are 4 canines and 14 molars. With these sharp fangs, the cat can kill the bird or the mouse that it has seized, after a dazzling leap which can reach up to five times its height. Moreover, this small feline is endowed with all the attributes of the perfect hunter, including an optimal eyesight and a very fine-tuned hearing. Its whiskers are so sensitive that they can identify the presence of a prey hidden in his hole. In the twilight, these few hairs are more precious to him than sight! Like large cats, the cat attacks prey larger than himself, and it is the only predator that has allowed itself to be domesticated by man.

FUR

*From her blond and brown fur,
comes a sweet perfume [...]*
CHARLES BAUDELAIRE

The cat's entire body is covered with hair, except the nose, the udders and the bottom of its feet. These hairs grow from the skin, inside tiny openings called "follicles." They are bushier on the belly, where there are 200 hairs per square millimeter against 100 on the back. These hairs are of three kinds: guard hair, the covering hair of varying length according to the feline breeds; the hair of the undercoat that also provides protection, and a final undercoat that is soft and curly. As for the cat's hair cycle, it is linked not only to genetic factors, but also to the environment, temperature and lighting. All of these different hairs form the cat's fur coat: it is a protection against cold and heat, but also against bacteria.

THE CAT AND THE WOMAN

*When my fingers caress at leisure your head
and your elastic back [...] I see my wife in spirit.*
Charles Baudelaire

There are many things in common between cats and women. Poets, writers and painters have never ceased to make the connection between the two. Both represent gentleness, but also carry in them a wild force which manifests itself suddenly. Never disturb the cat surrounded by her kittens, for she's more of a tigress! In the same way, one is careful not to upset the versatile woman who, quick to sting, passes from serenity to aggressiveness. Literature has seized upon the mystery of this unpredictable behavior, to which sensuality is added. Thus, Baudelaire, in *"Le Chat"* (*Les Fleurs du mal*, 1861), expresses his thoughts for his muse while caressing his cat. It is undeniable that the lascivious positions of the little feline evoke the attitudes of the woman waiting for love. The soft meowing of the pussy also has the power to soften and move, just like the voice, which is inscribed in the inventory of female seduction weapons. Finally, when one considers the maternal behavior of both the woman and the cat, one discerns many similar facts and gestures.

THE CAT AND THE CHILD

Something that our mind cannot understand or grasp after long effort, must not be necessary...
CLARIS DE FLORIAN

The strength of the bonds that unite the cat and the child comes from the resemblance between these two little beings. Both invent nonsense and quarrel. For the kitten, the child is an ideal accomplice. For nothing rejoices it more than the world of play! The little cat pounces on the ball or knocks over the construction sets. For the little girl, it turns into a doll and is transported in a pram. A faithful friend, the cat waits for the end of the school day, settles on the desk and encourages the children to do their homework. It is also the ideal animal for a single child, because it is a small companion for any moment of the day, bearing witness to drama and sorrow. Its sweetness and understanding appear as great consoling virtues for the toddler. An indispensable friend, this good little devil will have but one request: that you respect his precious sleep

THE MATERNAL INSTINCT

Her black son, [...] she caresses him and says the only word she knows: "Prrou, prrou ..."
COLETTE

Maternal love is exemplary in cats: she fulfills not only her role as a nurse but also that of a model mother, with the affection she showers on her kittens and the education she gives them. From breast-feeding to grooming the new-born, the cat has hardly any respite: lying on the flank in a nursing position, she encourages her young to suckle by placing a paw on them. Fully devoted to her offspring, she devotes 90% of her time and only abandons the family nest for food ... very soon, the kittens are meow again in hunger and because of their first drama (the weakest are pushed away by the strong ones who give themselves the best teats. But in the organization of siblings, the mother does not intervene. She is content to comfort the weakest. Yet she ensures an constant watch, which will be accompanied by the first lessons. She gives the example, corrects the undisciplined, showing a sense of pedagogy unmatched in the animal kingdom. These lessons are crucial for the little feline, who will not be separated from his mother before the age of three months, sometimes even more.

BETWEEN CATS AND DOGS

If I prefer cats to dogs, it is because there are no police cats.
Jean Cocteau

Cats and dogs doesn't necessarily mean brawling and clawing. Living together is possible, and the complicity between these two pets can often run deep. When they grow up together under the same roof, success is guaranteed. If the bond is not established spontaneously, it is because their language does not rely on the same animal codes. When the dog wags its tail, it is because he pleased or friendly. The cat sees in this same movement a sign of aggression. In the world of cats, the act of moving the tail translates into a state of nervousness. Another case is to be noted, equally frequent: when raising the paw, the dog offers his friendship. In feline language, this movement has another meaning. This is a warning, or even a threat. It is thus a deaf dialogue between the two animals. But after the series of misunderstandings, the cat and the dog can become good friends. Breed is not without influence in the success of their relations. The bulldog, however impressive, is inoffensive with the cat. The pug, on the other hand, is ferocious only with its voice, but what terror it strikes in the heart of a cat!

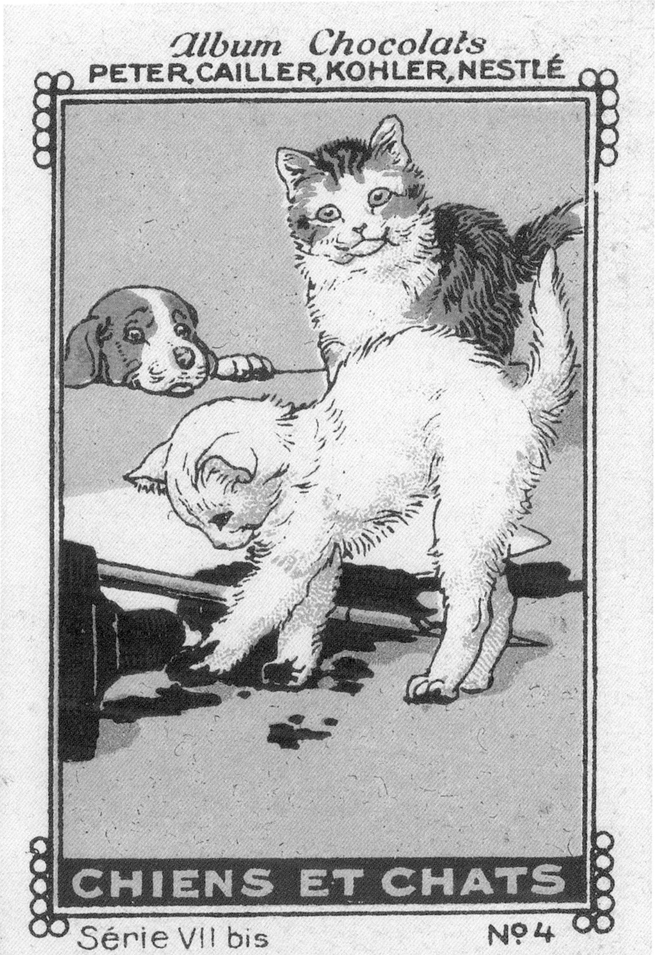
Album Chocolats
PETER, CAILLER, KOHLER, NESTLÉ
CHIENS ET CHATS
Série VII bis
N° 4

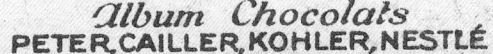

CAT EYES

*His yellow eyes left only a slit to
coin the gold of nighttime.*
PABLO NERUDA

The cat has eyes as round as the moon or almond-shaped. Depending on its breed, the color of the iris is light or dark. Set at the age of four months, it can be copper, as in the Chartreux, emerald green, as in the Persian chinchilla, or sapphire blue, as in the Siamese. Cat eyes face forward - not laterally as in other carnivores, such as the wolf and the dog, or in certain herbivores, such as the horse. This frontal position allows the little feline to fully appreciate depth. It also has good peripheral vision, which allows it to see around him without moving its head - immobility is part of the predator's strategy! Thus, its visual field is superior to that of man (180 degrees versus 160). This is why nothing can escape the cat: if it observes a prey (bird or mouse), it can evaluate with great precision the distance at which it is between 2 and 6 meters. This piercing view is an indispensable asset to this great hunter.

THE GAZE

*I see with astonishment the fire of
his pale pupils, clear lanterns, living opals.*
CHARLES BAUDELAIRE

The expression in the cat's gaze is not easy to interpret. The effects of light and those of the mood must not be confused. On the defensive, the cat has enlarged pupils. This is the case in particular in the presence of a stranger. When he is at peace, in the company of its master, for example, they are almost closed. In the dark, the pupils dilate. In the light, they become a simple slit. Moreover, when the cat looks at a distant object, it looks like round black puddles that grow larger. If the object approaches, they contract. The dilated pupils also indicate that the cat is hungry. In this case, their size can quadruple or quintuple in one second. Finally, the eyes of the cat may sometimes seem unexpected: it closes its eyes as well when it surrenders to ecstasy as when it loses a fight.

NIGHT VISION

The Chinese see the time in the eyes of cats.
CHARLES BAUDELAIRE

The eye of the cat, like that of man, consists of cones and rod cells. The former are used to distinguish colors. The latter play an essential role in the understanding of forms and movements in the middle of the night. These rods are extremely sensitive to even weak light. If the cat sees at night, it is precisely because these cells are in the majority. The cat also has a high-performance night vision thanks to the *tapetum lucidum* in its eye. This kind of reflecting carpet, located behind the retina, sends back the light. Thanks to it, the slightest glow turns into true light. The cat can then be seen making big eyes, for the more the light diminishes, the bigger and rounder the pupil becomes.

THE MASTER OF THE HOUSEHOLD

*I am the Cat who walks by himself,
and all places are alike to me.*
RUDYARD KIPLING

Like its bigger feline cousins, the cat is very attached to its territory. It has a vital need for a private domain. To point out to his that he is the master of a place, he has an efficient means, the marking, the form of which varies according to the mood or the environment (urine jet, secretions emitted by friction of the body, or by scratching). Thus, when it is about to mark its territory, it takes on a clumsy attitude, with the right legs and the tail erect and agitated with tremors, then sprinkles all the vertical objects - tree trunks, low walls, flower basins. The passing feline, which smells pheromones, deduces a multitude of information: a veritable identity card of the owner of the premises (age, sex, sexual state), nature of the message (time of passage, authorization or ban on entering). The cat divides its territory into zones, where it applies the rule of unity of action, place and time. Here he hunts (and eats) at his hours; here he rests; In the distance, he charms his sweetheart. Its hunting ground is classified as a forbidden reserve, and it does not share its resting place, where it likes to bask in the sun. On the other hand, any cat in heat is welcome during the love season.

BODY LANGUAGE

*Man is civilized to the extent that
he understands the cat.*
BERNARD SHAW

With its body, the cat declares war or makes peace. It also communicates its intentions. Very angry with an opponent, it walks sideways, salivating. On the lookout, body in a ball, head tucked into its shoulders and its tail agitated by slight lateral movements. The different positions of the tail deliver a dozen messages. If the animal is furious, it pins the air with it. It bristles it to signify its aggressiveness and puts it in arc when it is on the defensive. A straight tail is a welcoming sign. If it is slightly curved, it is because the cat shows a keen interest in what is going on in the surroundings. Moreover, a tail hel to side is to declare his flame to his sweetheart, and the tail swings when it sees a bird behind the window or plays with a companion. The cat also expresses its moods with its back. When threatening, his back seems to swell, with the hair on end. On the other hand, a rounded back indicates that it is content and wants caresses. Finally, to show friendship to the master, the cat gives its paw, as the mother cat does with her young.

VERBAL LANGUAGE

*— Mouek mouek mouek… Ma-a-a-a… Ma-a-a-a …,
says Saha, addressing a small captive caterpillar.*
COLETTE

One decodes seven messages in the cat's vocal language: anger, which causes him to groan; Fear, which he reveals in throat noises; suffering, which appears in its acute meowings; an invitation to follow it when it issues an ascending trill; frustration, which it exteriorizes by a rattle of the teeth; friendship, expressed by the purr; a demand for attention associated with its almost chirping when it is a kitten. To express all these feelings, the cat uses different degrees of vocalizations. For anger, for example, it uses hissing, "sss," a low-intensity sound. This war cry is extremely effective. One immediately thinks of serpents! The animal also uses spitting, "fft," the rumble, "grr," and the growl, "eo." It has mastered the art of intimidating the enemy without ever raising his voice! High intensity sounds, for their part, are reserved for intraspecific language, which allows communication between congeners. Finally, the feline repertoire includes sometimes incongruous cries that are unsuited to the situation. Compared to the song of love that is chirped, the hiccupped cry directed at the the bird out the window seems very light.

MEOWING

That voice forms into drops, trickles
Into the depths of my being,
Fills me like harmonious verse
And gladdens me like a philtre.
CHARLES BAUDELAIRE

Among all sorts of vocalizations that characterize the cat's repertoire (from sixty-three to a hundred, according to specialists), meowing falls into the category of high intensity sounds and vowels. Thus, during a fight, the cat emits a wide variety of meowings, keeping the mouth wide open. This feline partition, a true pandemonium, is usually called caterwauling. It contains as many feverish sexual undertones as it does rustic demonstrations of the cat's combativeness. There is a yelp of pain from the female feline at the end of intercourse, when the male withdraws- nothing like the soft cooing precedes the sexual act!

PURRING

I studied many philosophers and several cats.
The wisdom of cats is infinitely superior.
Hippolyte Taine

This innate language, which appears from the first feeding, is the particularity of felines. It is explained by the passage of air during their respiratory movements. The contraction of the muscles of the larynx, which takes place thirty times per second, effectively halts the air and produces this muffled whirring. The "brn" sound is produced during the inspiratory movement, the "rhn" sound during the expiratory movement. This phonetic variation is a function of the speed of the air. The purrs are emitted in the closed mouth and correspond to soft, brief and not very intense sounds. They come in four notes, which translate as "mr-br," for the purring, "e-mr," for the call, "me," for thankfulness, and "mmr" for greeting. As an adult, the cat purrs as soon as it is caressed, approached or talked to. With its fellows, it purrs to show its good mood. Curiously, it uses the same language in painful situations, such as when it gives birth or during a visit to the veterinarian.

SLEEP

*It is not blood circulating in its veins,
but linden infusion.*
Jean-Louis Hue

The cat spends 60% of its time sleeping. A serene atmosphere or a gentle warmth are enough to make it sink quickly into the arms of Morpheus. In its sleep, the cat has its muscles relaxed, eyes closed, and smell and hearing are inoperative. Only mustaches vibrate. Unlike men, it is not caught in a continuous asleep, but it accumulates naps, between active phases (games and hunting). Sleep is therefore not at all rest. It even intrigued researchers who, since the early 1980^s, regarded it as an enigma. The sleep of the cat takes place in fact in four phases. Analyzes using electroencephalograms detected the phase of falling sleep (very short), that of light sleep (half the time), that of deep sleep (moment when the cat relaxes its muscles) and that of paradoxical sleep-REM- (a quarter of the time). During this last phase, that of dreams, the cat adopts a surprising attitude. Instead of being motionless, it executes jerky movements. Light jumps, quivering mustaches and the trembling of paws are therefore clues that the cat is dreaming.

Reward of Merit

Presented to

Teacher.

GROOMING

Aesthetic perfection and technical perfection combine in the movements of the cat.
KONRAD LORENZ

Twice a day, the cat goes through a complete self-grooming session and polishes during the day with brief and regular touch-ups. Contrary to certain expressions then, cats are in fact quite clean! The cat begins its grooming by wetting a front paw with its tongue - the second serves as its support. And as if it had a washcloth, it then rubs its whole head, passes the paw behind the ears and uses it to clean its cheeks and chin. With a change of paw, it follows the same scenario, but on the other side. Then, to wash its breastplate and the back of the shoulders, it stretches its head upwards and curves its neck. To lick its flanks, its resorts toits rasping tongue, and, to undo the knots of fur, puts its teeth into it. Finally, in an inelegant posture, it switches to intimate hygiene and cleans the genitals. It then bites its hind legs without mercy in order to get out every last stain and piece of dirt and grime.

THE ORDINARY SENSES

He seemed to me just formed to sympathise
With timid mice : for he has got an ear,
The very shape of ours, or very near.
JEAN DE LA FONTAINE

The cat is endowed with five ordinary senses of high performance. Its nose includes two chemoreceptors (nerve cells informing the brain), as in all mammals, as well as Jacobson's organ, which contains no less than 200 million sensory cells specializing in the detection of pheromones. With his hypersensitive hearing, the cat captures the sounds that we cannot. It can hear the faintest noises, such as the trotting of a mouse, because its hearing is equipped with an amplification device. It thus perceives sound frequencies reaching 100 kHz, that is to say 100,000 cycles per second, whereas the average perceived by humans is at 17 kHz. The cat also has a piercing view and at night it can see as in broad daylight. Its sense of touch, superior to that of the dog, is exerted through the pads at the soles of the feet and five skin regions: the face, the muzzle, the chin, the belly, the flanks and the ano-genital region. Finally, the cat has a very fine sense of taste which makes it selective in the choice of its food.

THE SIXTH SENSE

The cat is satisfied with being:
it is the verb which it conjugates the best.
Louis Nucéra

In addition to the five ordinary senses, the cat has four other senses that allow him to perform great performances: the sense of temperature, that of balance, that of orientation and that of time. The last two are referred to as "sixth sense." Thus, the Swedish philosopher Emmanuel Swedenborg (1688-1772) considers these animals as "living compasses," led by "spheres absolutely unknown to man." We also noticed that the cat knows perfectly the schedules of the movements of the house, which gives the impression that he knows how to read the time. He alerted his master if he did not wake by accident, and he waited behind the door, always at the same time, his young companion on his return from school. To explain this regularity, it is assumed that the cat uses the solar hour. Surprisingly, the cat is also there when you cross the door at an unusual hour. This makes some say that he possesses a gift of prescience, also called "psi trailing." Others go so far as to say that the cat can foresee catastrophes, foresee the death of its relatives and communicate by thought.

THE GROOMING OF THE KITTENS

The cat, my model, the pussy, my friend.
Colette

The first sensation of a kitten arriving in the world is a lick. The mother greeted him in fact with grooming, licking him vigorously on the muzzle, then on the whole body. It thus removes the impurities that obstruct its nostrils to gives it every chance to breathe. Shortly afterwards, it favors the ano-genital area. A vital gesture without which the little one would be condemned to death, for he could neither urinate nor defecate. The kitten is thus familiar with cleanliness at the dawn of its existence. Until the age of five weeks, he acquires the know-how to carry out his grooming. It learns the methods of cleansing and nibbling with the claws on the fur. It is also through the licking that the little cat, awkward at first, discovers his body and measures its suppleness. If there is a place he can not access, then he counts on his brothers and sisters to help him. Grooming therefore is not limited to cleanliness, it also serves in communication.

THE FIRST DAYS

I was born in a barrel [...] The first eight days, everything seemed pink to me.
HIPPOLYTE TAINE

All shiny from ear to tail, the kitten measures about ten centimeters at birth. And grimacing, it moves by crawling. Its weight is then of barely 100 grams. Only a few minutes old, he is able, although he is blind, to go to his mother's belly. It can also already coordinate the udder with its front legs to pull the milk. This is the sign of the establishment of the vestibular system, that is, the balance, which develops after the tactile system. After a few sucking movements, the kitten falls asleep. Crawling, sucking, squealing and sleeping for the most part of its time is the newborn's program! At one week, the kitten's eyes begin to open. It has already been able to assert its personality: it has chosen its favorite udder, and none of the brothers and sisters has the right to take its place. Then the first steps it makes, stumbling on the fifteenth day, push it towards all that is new: the sounds, the shapes. Without ever going away from its mother, he also sometimes ventures to play with his brothers and sisters.

THE FIRST GAMES

It is a little black cat, cheeky as a page.
I let him play on my table, often.
Edmond Rostand

Alone or with his brothers and sisters, the young cat spends his time playing. From the third week on, it plays games. One sees the kitten, belly in the air and legs slightly folded, plowing the opponent and dragging him into the battle with strong paws. Other games: one is standing, the other lying on the ground. There is also one where it's all about impressing the rival, with the arched back and the puffy hair. Then comes the game of the side step, followed immediately by the hunting games (the hunt, the pursuit, the tackle). When the game of combat comes, a disagreement between kittens is solved by a duel, in which the two enemy brothers turn into boxers. In reality, fighting is an educational game, where everything ends with cuddling and licks. There is also the game of hallucinations, which consists in catching an invisible gnat. At eight weeks, the kitten is devoted to individual games. It is the time when he confuses objects and prey. He takes a ball of wool for a mouse, a cork stopper hanging on a door handle for a bird, a slipper for a rabbit and a paper ball for a fish.

LEARNING HUNTING

The cat invented "pigeon vole."
DESMOND MORRIS

In the life of a cat, playing is essential to learn to hunt. At three weeks of age, the kitten engages in a battle against its mother for fun. She herself introduces her kitten to the hunt by swinging he tail, which the kitten catches by reflex. At one month, the kitten taps a dead mouse (or a fly) brought by its mother. By practicing the attack, he advances a little in the techniques of hunting, at the same time that he learns the gestures of survival. At five weeks, he jumps, grabs and brings the objects back. This foreshadowing of the hunt is declined in three specific games: those of the mouse, the bird and the fish. The mouse is a ball, towards which it rushes to catch it with its paws to immobilize it. The bird is represented by a cap suspended from a string. The fish takes shape in a ball of paper that the kitten throws over it. Finally, the kitten invents imaginary prey: he ambushes a dustbunny or tracks the shadow of his tail, which he takes for a mouse. In the evening he walks sideways with his tail erect, and rushes to the pursuit of nothingness. It is indeed "at the time of the lamps," according to Colette's expression, that the hunter instinct of the kitten is best practiced.

THE FIGHTS

If you want to paint men, first observe the cats.
ALDOUS HUXLEY

The defense of territory and the rivalry between males are the main causes of the fights between cats. The first is the most spectacular. It takes place in four phases. First, the attacked cat is alone and spits. His pupils are reduced to a single stroke, his coat is bristling and his tail erect. Second, he makes the "breed across," propelling himself by leaps perpendicularly to his opponent. Thirdly, it only happens when it comes close to the intruder and projects urine. Fourth is the assault: with teeth and claws, it drags the enemy out of the territory. Feline love is also a source of fights. It is always the female who chooses her suitor. This does not prevent the males from wanting to impose themselves at all costs and to show off to the lady. To start the fight, each of the opponents has his eyes set on the other and tries to intimidate them. The hair bristling and the tail voluminous, they then wrestle one another. The winner will not always earn the favors of the beautiful. For the prize goes to the more clever of the two.

THE SOCIALIZATION OF THE KITTEN

The cat is a philosophic beast who does not place his affections to the daze.
Théophile Gautier

At home or in the garden, the kitten meets its congeners, crosses other species and opens to contacts of all kinds. Thus, between four and eight weeks, he becomes autonomous. At one month, he began to distance himself from his mother and became isolated. If he hears a noise that surprises him or encounters an unusual object, he no longer calls for help in spite of his terror. Immediately on the defensive, he spits, the body in an arc of circle, the inflamed eye and the claws in sight. During this period, thirsty for adventures and ripe for the conquest of his environment, he does not leave the clan. At five weeks, he goes to meet adult cats, and he returns to the family home only if hunger draws him back. He is then able to leave his mother permanently. At two months, the kitten is ready to make friends. The relations between cats are very beneficial, although, at the beginning, the spitting and hissing is de rigueur. Without fear or reproach, the kitten does not shrink from anything. He tries, for example, to intimidate a dog, whatever its size or type. And at this stage, it loves to cuddle in its master's arms, confusing it with its mother.

CAT DIALOGUE

Saha!
Me-rraing! Replied the cat, sharply.
Is it my fault if you are hungry?
Colette

The more we talk with our cats, the more they express themselves. Education is not without some influence on the animal's chatter. With his master, the cat emits soft sounds. Mouth closed, it is expressed in vowels. It is his way of attracting attention, giving his approval or showing his gratitude. The cat makes a "meow" sound, if he has any worries, says "mraou" to ask for the door to be opened and "maraâou" to demand that it be opened on the spot! And if he is denied something, he grumbles "maw," complains while doing "meaou" or gets angry while grumbling "waw." The feline prolixity also varies according to the age, circumstances, personality and breed of the cat. In general, short-haired cats are more talkative than others. Siamese, Oriental, Burmese, Tonkinese and Bengal are among the most voluble in this category. The Persian, the only long-haired cat, does not often hear the sound of his own voice. As for cats with long hair, such as the sacred of Burma and the Norwegian, the cat's got their tongue.

OUTDOOR LIFE

At night all the cats are gray.
PROVERB

In the garden, the cat hunts down its footed meal. Lying on the ground with baited breath, he spent hours watching the mice. He jumps, then knocks them down with his paw on the back of the neck. The first prey of the day is always a trophy. He places the mouse on the doorstep and meows at the top of its voice so that its master may recognize and appreciate its prowess. The victim is more often a mouse than a sparrow, because the cat lets go of 90% of the birds that it has been able to seize and they escape. In the garden, he also regains his primitive freedom and reproduces the gesture of his ancestor, the wild cat. He wanders among the shrubs, breathes in the perfumes, chews the leaves, scrapes the earth and claws on the trunks of trees. A true botanist, he also sniffs plants, which he appreciates depending on their scent.

INDOOR LIFE

I love cats because I love my house and they become, little by little, the visible soul.
Jean Cocteau

The indoor cat does not lack activities, between grooming, observation, naps and games. But after having lived for millennia in nature, the animal, enclosed within four walls, must find the tbreeds of its natural setting. He must be able to climb, nest himself in the hiding-places represented by the cabinets or his quilted basket, and use his claws. It can not be happy without a cat tree, from where it has all the time to observe its imaginary prey and to capture them ... in his dreams! Strings and stoppers hanging low allow it to grip and jump. Paper balls are the most exciting toys for the cat hunter. He also likes to tease felted characters such as socks and balls. The well-being of the domestic cat comes down to a gentle and calm framework, adequate food and proper hygiene. These basic principles are also enshrined in the Animal Charter, enacted within the framework of the Nature Protection Act. This 1976 text recommends that the living conditions of the animal be close to the natural environment, and it must eat according to its specific needs and be well treated. We can not do less for our feline friends!

AT HOME

*It is an animal necessary to an interior,
it complements it.*
Stéphane Mallarmé

At home, the cat has the art of recreating its wild paradise. As in nature, it delimits its territory in five spaces. It occupies all of them, at different times of the day, depending on its activity. The rest area, the dining area, the toilet, the playground and the observation post make up its kingdom. Here, there is no notion of surface, since the hunting domain of its natural environment does not exist. The size of the dwelling to be shared with the master is therefore unimportant for the cat. Whatever the architecture of the dwelling, it always manages to make it its territory. Certainly he likes a two-storey house where he can climb and go down stairs, sit on the landing and watch the comings and goings, keeping an eye on the garden. But a cozy apartment makes it just as happy, and it makes a realm out of a simple studio. According to its breed, the cat has its privileged places. The shelves and the cornices of the cupboards are the happiness of the Abyssinian, always looking for height. The Japanese bobtail, a great lover of water, hangs out in the bathroom. The Chartreux, a quiet type, spends his life in the library, and the Persian would not leave his sofa for an empire.

A DELICATE PALATE

I drank to the alleys, and never had sweet milk seemed so sweet.
ÉMILE ZOLA

Delicate, the cat tastes food with caution. It is the smell of food that guides him in his choices. He tests his meal by smelling his plate, then, guided and reassured by his flair, he tries the first bite. Preferring to cry famine than to eat with reluctance, such could be the motto of this delicate palate. That the freshness of a food leaves something to be desired, the cat will manifest a profound disgust. And if an unusual chemical scent emerges from his dish, the cat has already turned on his heels. He also has his preferences in the menu that is proposed to him. Carnivorous, he is not a big meat eater. He likes green vegetables and pasta or rice, three ingredients that must be found in any balanced meal. The liver is synonymous with feast. The fish is often ranked number one in the chart of its favorite meals. But he disdains catfish, too soft and with a particularly strong smell. Cod, with firm flesh and a rather neutral taste, seduces this fine mouth much more. The cat is also faithful to its youthful eating habits. This explains its strong attraction for milk, a drink of its early days. However, it is said to be more focused on acid, bitter and salty. In fact, it has very varied tastes.

THE CAT AND THE PLANTS

Oh ! The pretty flower in the window!
Yes it is a small white poppy. [...]
It is not a flower, it is a cat...
COLETTE

The cat ignores the risks it incurs by falling under the charm of plants. To get to know them better, the little curious one approaches, nibbles on them, and chew and chews. Leaves and berries, stems and flowers, which it enjoys without restraint. Some plants are toxic though. Whether in the apartment or in the garden, the cat is not immune to serious poisoning, which gives it diarrhea, and repeated vomiting. Outside, he must be wary of yew, oleander, aristolochia, cytisea and ivy. At home, about twenty plants leave a bad spell for the felines. Eye irritations and skin burns are all effects caused by croton, rubber, ficus, poinsettia and dieffenbachia. Also, to the allamanda, a small shrub with yellow flowers, chrysanthemum, which causes allergic dermatitis! The cat is still at risk of kidney disease due to philodendron, cardiovascular damage caused by rhododendron and cyclamen, and nervous disorders caused by the apple tree. Mistletoe, holly, azalea and aucuba are also dangerous for this budding botanist.

SOLITUDE

To marvel at being able to share my house with these little tigers [...].
KONRAD LORENZ

The cat, after the age of six months, adapts well enough to solitude. It has the advantage of not expressing itself to manifest its boredom, unlike the dog, who barks. Nevertheless, it doesn't hesitate to show its discontent if its remains alone for too long. A stained sofa, an upside-down vase of flowers, and above all linen wet with a few drops of urine diffusing an unbearable and tenacious odor ... such are the manifestations of his vengeance. Locked up between four walls, the cat is accustomed to the absence of its master. His ability to adapt and his predisposition to calm and observation allow him to experience this isolation more easily than the dog, for example. However, the curiosity of the cat must be fully satisfied: it must always enjoy a view on the outside. A window without a shutter, with a curtain which it can lift, in order to gaze at the horizon, is the ideal arrangement for it to be able to observe.

THE PUREBRED

Come my beautiful cat, on my heart in love.
CHARLES BAUDELAIRE

Unlike the alley cat, the purebred cat has a pedigree: its physique must correspond to the standard established by the breeding committee of an association. This ideal description serves as a reference for the official recognition of a cat breed. It is composed of a scale of points, from 5 to 100, in which all parts of the cat, the body, the eyes, the head and the fur, receive a value. Sometimes, a cat breed has several standards, which vary according to the judgments of the various felinophilic world bodies: the International Feline Federation (FIFA), the Cat Fancier's Association (CFA) and the International Cat Association (Tica). When his pedigree is confirmed, the purebred cat is inscribed in the official book of feline origins, which is recognized throughout the world. This is the sine qua non for a cat to enter competitions and exhibitions, get titles and become an international champion. When a cat does not meet the requirements for competitions, it is sold as a pet cat.

THE COMPETITION CAT

Powdered, curled, perfumed, trimmed, adjusted and rendered more beautiful than Adonis [...].
MADAME D'AULNOY

The contest cat must meet the criteria demanded by the felinophilic authorities, sport a beautiful and perfectly maintained coat, look great and be healthy. It must also conform to the breed standard and be free of deformity and defects. Enrollment in the Official Book of Feline Origins is mandatory, unless it is included in the Register of Experimental Registration. This document lists cats whose genealogy or breed is not recognized by the official book. Before it passes this examination, the cat is groomed thoroughly, vaccinated, dewormed and electronically identified. To compete, he must still have passed the sanitary control, his owner must have paid the registration fees and his papers have been checked. It is only after that that the candidate is installed in his exhibition cage. Nothing then escapes the critical eye of the judges. For appearance is not enough! The contest cat must indeed be very sociable and accept to be held in the arms without resisting or hissing. Over the course of competitions he passes from one class to another according to his gender and age.

SILHOUETTE

Dear Beauty, nature can not make a cat as perfect as you.
HONORÉ DE BALZAC

The purebred cat is distinguished especially by its silhouette. Thus, the size indications vary from "small" to "very large" - for example, from bengal and californian spangled cat - to "medium" and "large." The weight is always given precisely. The smallest of the purebred cats, the singapura, weighs not more than 3 kilos, while the heavier one, the maine coon, exceeds 10 kilos, and the heaviest can reach up to 14 kilos. In addition, there are three types of morphology of purebred cats:

- the brebiline type, or cobby, is distinguished by its stocky body, its large rounded head, and its short tail, as in the Persian;
- the medium type is characterized by a rectangular body, an average tail and a balanced head. It is subdivided into three genera: the semi-cobby, that is to say semi-collected, like the British shorthair; The semiforeign, with the medium skeleton, like the European one; The long and substantial, that is to say with the long and powerful body, like the Norwegian or the sacred cat of Burma. The "foreign" silhouette concerns the lightest medium-sized format, like the Abyssinian;
- the longiline or oriental type is determined by a long tubular body, such as that of the Siamese.

THE COAT

The breast, the belly, and the legs were as white as the down of a swan.
Pierre Loti

The color palette of the coats is immense, because within the same breed there are several varieties of hues. The furs range from black to blue to chocolate, gray, red, cream, white, bicolour, partiallu colored and silver, not to mention coats with pattern, such as point coloration in the Siamese, and the tabby, in the European or the Persian. More specifically, the tabby cat presents itself with blotched, thin stripes, spotted, or stripes only on the legs, collar and tail. The fur can also be both "torbie": tabby and tortoise shell with two colors and white or blue.

THE RANGE OF BREEDS

In societies, cats will be sought.
François-Augustin de Paradis de Moncrif

There are nearly seventy official breeds, recognized by independent clubs or attached to the French feline federation. They fall into three categories. The short hairs are forty-four in number: abyssinian, american curl, american shorthair, american wirehair, asian, bengal, japanese bobtail, bombay, british shorthair, burmese American shaman, burmese, californian rex, californian spangled cat, ceylan, Chartreux, chausie, cornish rex, devon rex, donskoy, european, exotic shorthair, german rex, Havana, korat, kurilian bobtail, laperm, manx, egyptian mau, munchkin cat, ocicat, peterbald, pixie bob, russian (blue, black, white), savannah, Scottish fold, selkirk rex, siamese, singapura, snowshoe, sokoke, sphynx, thai, tonkinois. There are twenty-two milongs: american bobtail, american curl, turkish angora, balinese, japanese bobtail, medium-haired british, cymric, highland fold, kurilian Medium-haired bobtail, medium-haired laperm, maine coon, nebelung, norwegian, medium-haired pixie bob, sacred Burma, ragdoll, long-haired selkirk rex, Siberian, Somali, Tiffany, Turkish Lake Van, York Chocolate. The long hair includes only one breed: the Persian.

HISTORY OF BREEDS

You will thus show yourself only in your beauty.
HONORÉ DE BALZAC

The only cat that is at the origin of the feline nobility is ... the alley cat. Curiously, in competitions his only title is "house cat." This great genitor, however, has shaped the feline geography in the world, swarming from one country to another thanks to the sailors who brought it on board to hunt ship rats. Wherever he went, this adventurer quickly became acclimated, and from his crosses with the indigenous cats were born different breed. Then the breeds evolved thanks to the intervention of man, who arranged the marriages, so to speak. In order to achieve this, a long-term breeding exercise had to be carried out on several lines. The aim was to obtain solid breeds, different from each other, and to keep them safe from inadequate cross-breeding or hereditary diseases. The purebred cat began to impose itself at the first feline exhibition, organized in London, at the Crystal Palace, in 1871. At the time we didn't yet speak of breeds or breeds, but of "classes." It was not until the very beginning of the twentieth century that sixteen breeds were designated by the authorities of the felinophilic world. Today, there are nearly seventy officially recognized breeds.

EXOTIC CATS

Stuffed and stained just like the other,
like the defunct Moumoutte of Senegal.
Pierre Loti

In the category of short-haired cats, one finds the Egyptian. Venerated in antiquity, it was introduced in Italy in 1953 by a Russian princess. In a silver dress, bronze or smoke, it has an M on the forehead and rings on the tail. The Ceylon cat, discovered in 1984 in Sri Lanka by an Italian veterinarian, wears a tabby dress, with a black, blue, red and cream pattern. The Abyssinian does not come from Abyssinia (present-day Ethiopia), as its name might suggest, but from Southeast Asia. His coat is particular, each hair has three strips of color. The Japanese bobtail, which appeared in the country of the rising sun in the tenth century, has its tail in a pompom shape. The korat bears the name of a province of Thailand, where it is known since the sixteenth century. This lucky cat is in silver gray uniform blue. The Siamese with point coloration, was born in the kingdom of Siam, now Thailand. The oriental is the cat that has the richest variety of dresses, four hundred colors in total. The singapura, which takes its name from the island of Singapore, is the smallest of cats. Its scintillating coat is unique, with only one pattern and one color, sepia. The sokoke, in shiny tabby marbled dress, lives in the forest of Sokoke district, Kenya.

THE PERSIAN

The Persian cat, thrown like a marabout scarf on the edge of my window.
COLETTE

The Persian wears a thick and long fur, which is essential to surviving the rugged climate of Asia Minor. He lived in the city of Ankara (in present-day Turkey), the birthplace of the Angora cat. However, the Persian was discovered in Persia by the Italian explorer Pietro della Valle, who brought him back to Europe in 1620. In the eighteenth century, the French naturalist Buffon (1707-1888) painted a scientific portrait of this cat in his *Histoire naturelle*: The short and heavy silhouette, the strong firm legs, the broad, round feet, the rounded forehead and the full cheeks. In the nineteenth century, the Persian held the spotlight: at the first feline exhibition in 1871 in London, Queen Victoria was seduced by the so-called "prince of cats." Majestic in its vaporous coat, the Persian is the only long-haired breed of the feline. Since 1967, the Persian type is recognized in the category of short hair under the name of exotic shorthair. The latter, who does not need a daily grooming, has the same wardrobe of a hundred colors like the Persian: white, black, lilac, red, cream, bicolour, tabby, chinchilla, smoke, etc. Discreet and friendly, as well as of great serenity, the Persian is the model indoor cat.

THE SIAMESE

The ideal of calm is in a sitting cat.
JULES RENARD

The history of the Siamese is very old and is located in the Far East. As the name suggests, this cat has its cradle in Siam, the ancient kingdom that is presentday Thailand. Its elegant and slender silhouette illustrates the manuscripts of the *Book of Cat's Poems* (1350) found in the ancient Siamese capital, Ayuthia. This cat has inspired Buddhism, some beliefs about the cat survived until the nineteenth century. Thus, it was believed until that date that when a wise man died, his soul took refuge in the body of a cat and that it acceded to paradise only at the disappearance of the animal. Legends, which also play with reality, have transformed certain physical defects of the Siamese into extraordinary qualities. Thus, it was said that this cat, with its curved tail and sapphire eyes, had been affected with a squint, after having stared at length at the sacred objects of the royal temples of which he was in charge. The Siamese is also marked by a royal destiny: until 1927, it is the symbol of the soul of the kings of Thailand during the coronation ceremonies.

THE ANGORA

An angora fur, silky, clean, warm, feeling good, exquisite to brush and kiss.
Pierre Loti

In the eighteenth century a distinction was made between the Chartreux, the domestic cat and the Turkish angora. The Swedish naturalist Linnaeus (1707-1778) designates it under the scientific name of *Catus angorensis*. He named it in reference to the Turkish city of Ankara, now the capital of Turkey, from where the animal originated. As soon as the Italian explorer Pietro della Valle brought him back to Europe in the seventeenth century, angora became the stake of exchanges. Later, at the court of Louis XV., There was a boundless admiration for him. And we understand why: gbreedful, this cat sports a vaporous fur that, at the slightest displacement, sparkles like a shower of stars. His body is long and fine. Its small round feet let out tufts of interdigital hair. Its triangular head, with a straight nose, a firm chin and triangular ears adorned with hairs, harmonizes with its almond-shaped eyes, placed slightly obliquely. Its eyes are blue for a white coat, and amber for a tabby cat. The preference now goes to white angora.

THE CHARTREUX

The most beautiful work that nature ever made in the matters of cats [...].
JOACHIM DU BELLAY

The Chartreux forms one of the oldest feline breeds. It was introduced to Europe in 1254 by the Crusaders, who brought him back from the Middle East. Admired for its dense fur, it was saved by the monks of the Grande Chartreuse, who appreciated this excellent mouse hunter. It was thanks to the Léger sisters, who raised him in Belle-Île-en-Mer in the 1930s, that the Chartreux became famous. The breed was recognized in 1939. Today, the Chartreux is the favorite among short-haired cats. Its luminous robe is unique in the heart of the feline: uniform and without stain or shade, it ranges from light blue-gray to dark blue-gray. This cat has the same blue on its truffle, while its paws are pinkish-gray. With its trapezoidal head, triangular ears and large copper-colored eyes, it has "a waking air," as its standard (profile established by the felinophilic instances) underlines. Wide jowls, lustrous coat and massive body, the Chartreux represents the quiet strength.

THE SACRED CAT OF BURMA

And let me plunge into your beautiful eyes, mixed with metal and agate.
CHARLES BAUDELAIRE

According to legend, it was the guardian of the sacred temple of Lao-Tsun in Burma. This blue-eyed cat, whose semi-long fur never gets tangled, was born from the marriage between a white-haired Siamese and a long-haired cat. It was brought back to Europe in 1919 by the French diplomat Auguste Pavie and the British major of the Army of the Indies Russell Gordon. In 1926, it was presented at the International Feline Exhibition in Paris, where it was a great success. The breed was recognized forty years later in Great Britain; and in the United States in 1967. Elegant and majestic, sapphire blue eyes and silky coat, the sacred Burma has a long collar and a tail in panache. Its light fur, white to cream, contrasts with the points of its coat and its dark ends - ears, paws, tail and mask. This cat is also distinguished by its gloves in on each limb, and of a very pure hue of white; They form spurs at the back of the legs. Sometimes placid, sometimes exuberant, the sacred of Burma is perfectly balanced. He can be very talkative, like his cousin the Siamese, and also has a melodious voice.

CE N'EST PAS MOI QUE TU CARESSES
C'EST MA TASSE DE LAIT

THE EUROPEAN

But the cat only wants to be a cat and every cat is a cat from the mustache to the tail.

PABLO NERUDA

Descending from the European wild cat (*Felis sylvestris*) or the cat of the Near East (*Felis libyca*), the European has passed through history's cruelty: it was burned alive in the Middle Ages, eaten in stew and considered as a supporter of Satan. In 1925, the Cat Fancy (GCCF), the largest feline breeding organization in the UK, proposed that this street cat be recognized as a purebred cat, just as the Siamese or Persian. It thus gained its acclaim, but it was not until 1983 that the International Feline Federation (Fife) officially recognized the breed of this short-haired, tiger or speckled cat, united or bi-coloured. According to the standard that was then established, the European must be "free of all breed," that is to say never to have been crossed with another breed. Today, the European is charming with its appearance and personality. Independent and an eminent hunter, he has quick reflexes. He possesses an extraordinary ability to adapt. It is undoubtedly the most sociable of purebreds. Often confused with its cousin without pedigree, the alley cat, it is nevertheless less stocky than him and in no case does his coat show a white medallion around the neck.

THE NORWEGIAN

In a cat, you have a friend of very good company.
FRANÇOIS-AUGUSTIN DE PARADIS DE MONCRIF

The Norwegian (*skogkatt* in Norwegian) was discovered by the Vikings in Asia Minor and brought back to Europe on the drakkars in the eighth century. Its mission was to hunt rodents on these boats. This cat quickly became accustomed to the harsh climate of the Nordic countries: its coat thickens and is adorned with an abundant undercoat. It entered Nordic mythology in the thirteenth century. It is called the "Scandinavian fairy cat." Powerful and robust, it draws the chariot of Freyja, the goddess of Love, and Thor, the most powerful of the Scandinavian gods, fails to lift this big cat which can reach up to 9 kilos. In the twentieth century, the Norwegian became scarce. One sees him wandering in the woods, without law or master. It was not until 1977, after the official recognition of the breed, that its standard (an ideal profile established by the felinophilic authorities) is drafted: collar, crop, puffy pants, beaver tail, lynx hairs on the ears… He wears a semi-long coat, which can be of different colors: lilac, chocolate, cinnamon and fawn, but never point coloration. This great hunter, who is also a sportsman, likes to climb trees. It nevertheless adapts perfectly to life in the apartment. Mature at the age of four or five, he often expresses himself in his soft, singing voice.

THE MAINE COON

The powerful and gentle cats, pride of the house.
CHARLES BAUDELAIRE

The Maine coon is the oldest breed of American cats. According to legend, his parents are a wild cat from the state of Maine, on the east coast of the United States, and a racoon. In reality, it owes its existence to an angora from the Middle East and a short-haired American cat. In 1895, this Maine state cat won the supreme title of "best in show" at the feline exhibition held at Madison Square Garden, New York. However the breed is only officially recognized in North America in 1967. High on its legs and sturdy, the Maine coon can weigh up to 14 kilos. This giant body, long and rectangular, carries a cuneiform head, with large eyes. They sometimes come in tabby coats, or monocolored, tortoiseshell, silver, or smoke. This cat has no collar but a mane. Its large ears are furnished in long and fine hair; with long wisps of hair. Its paws are decorated with thick tufts of hair that act as snowshoes in the snow and palms in the water. Thanks to its smooth and waterproof fur, this cat swims at will and never gets cold when hunting in the garden in winter. Sumptuous and sweet, it is extremely cuddly and communicative. It is perfect for those who love cocooning!

CARING FOR CATS

You never choose a cat, it chooses you.
JACQUES LAURENT

Today, there are 10.7 million small cats in France, and the cat represents 37% of the pet market. In recent years, there has been a real revolution in how we feed them: a more balanced diet that is better adapted to each age and period of life (growth, castration, gestation, breastfeeding, old age). Cat food is also studied according to tastes, temperaments and certain diseases (obesity, diabetes). All these innovations, which result from major investment by research laboratories, have revolutionized veterinary science and feline nutrition. The market for animal hygiene is also quite important, since it has experienced in recent years a progression three times greater than that of food. Better cared for, cats avoid diseases but also acquire a well-being that inevitably improves their quality of life. Tattooed and vaccinated, they're followed by a veterinarian who keeps their papers up to date. Whether purebred or not, a cat now has an indisputably better place among men.

THE CAT OF THE 21ST CENTURY

*Looking at me in the eyes ...
indicated in his small head a whole
world of intelligent conceptions.*
Pierre Loti

The cat has earned man's esteem through his extraordinary adaptability to changes. It is one of the essential characteristics of this intelligent animal. In the course of its history, the cat has often seen its territory changed or altered. Nowadays forced to live in an apartment, even in a studio, it knows how to push back the limits of its domain. Its demands that all rooms and corners of the dwelling be accessible to him. Even the children's beds are open. Its art consists in not letting encroach on its borders. From a linguistic standpoint, the cat has become much more communicative. Because it is loved and considered a member of the family in its own right, it has developed a new mode of communication. It calls out to his master and asks if all is well. And to be better understood, it varies the intonations. It has long since been free from all the constraints of wild beasts and can now think of being a pet: being caressed, cuddled and cajoled.

BIBLIOGRAPHY AND SOURCES OF QUOTATIONS

Following each bibliographic reference are the pages where the quotations are mentioned in the book.

Aulnoy (Madame d'), *La Chatte blanche*, 1697 ; p. 36, 50, 138.
Balzac (Honoré de), « Peines de cœur d'une chatte anglaise », *Scènes de la vie privée et publique des animaux*, 1840-1842 ; p. 62, 140, 146.
Baudelaire (Charles), « L'Horloge », *Petits Poèmes en prose*, 1860 ; p. 90. « Le Chat », *Les Fleurs du mal*, 1861 ; p. 76, 78, 88, 98, 136, 158. « Les Chats », *Les Fleurs du mal*, 1861 ; p. 18, 24, 164.
Carroll (Lewis), *Alice in wonderland*, 1865 ; p. 68.
Champfleury, *Les Chats*, 1868 ; p. 14.
Chateaubriand (François-René de), *Lettre au comte de Marcellus*, 1817 ; p. 40.
Colette, *Les Vrilles de la vigne*, 1908 ; p. 44, 110. *La Paix chez les bêtes*, 1916 ; p. 82. *La Chatte*, 1933 ; p. 96, 122. « Autres bêtes », *Œuvres complètes*, 1949 ; p. 132, 150.
Du Bellay (Joachim), *Épitaphe d'un chat*, 1558 ; p. 156.
Florian (Claris de), « Le chat et le miroir », *Fables*, 1788 ; p. 80.
Gautier (Théophile), *Ménagerie intime*, 1869 ; p. 30, 120.
Genevoix (Maurice), *Rroû*, 1964 ; p. 34.
Hoffmann (Ernst Theodor Amadeus), *Murr the Cat's*, 1819 et 1821 ; p. 46.
Hue (Jean-Louis), *Le Chat dans tous ses états*, 2000 ; p. 48, 102.
Jammes (Francis), *Le Roman du lièvre*, 1902 ; p. 42.
Kipling (Rudyard), *The Cat that Walked by Himself*, 1902 ; p. 92.
Klingsor (Tristan), « Chanson du chat », *Florilège poétique*, 1955 ; p. 54.

La Fontaine (Jean de), « Le Cochet, le Chat et
le Souriceau » ; p. 106. « Le Chat, la Belette et le Petit Lapin »,
 Fables, 1664-1694 ; p. 60.
Laurent (Jacques), Les Bêtises, 1971 ; p. 166.
Lemaître (Jules), « À mon chat », Les Médaillons, 1896 ; p. 20.
Lorenz (Konrad), Tous les chiens, tous les chats, 1950 ;
 p. 104, 134.
Lorrain (Jean), Le Chat de Babaud Monnier, 1903 ; p. 32.
Loti (Pierre), Vies de deux chattes, 1907 ; p. 142, 148, 154, 168.
Maupassant (Guy de), Sur les chats, 1886 ; p. 12.
Méry (Fernand), Le Chat, 1966 ; p. 16.
Méry (Joseph), dans Correspondance de Victor Hugo, 1836-
 1882 et 1898 ; p. 72.
Mirbeau (Octave), Dingo, 1913 ; p. 70.
Montaigne (Michel de), Essais, 1580 ; p. 22
Morris (Desmond), Le Chat révélé, 1989 ; p. 116.
Neruda (Pablo), « Ode au chat », Le Quatrième Livre
 des odes, 1954 ; p. 86, 160.
Paradis de Moncrif (François-Augustin de), Histoires
 des chats, 1727 ; p. 56, 66, 144, 162.
Perrault (Charles), « Le Chat botté », Contes de ma mère
 l'Oye, 1697 ; p. 52.
Rollinat (Maurice), « Le chat », Les Névroses, 1883 ; p. 26.
Rostand (Edmond), « Le Petit chat », Les Musardises,
1911 ; p. 114.
Taine (Hippolyte), Vie et Opinions philosophiques d'un chat,
 1858 ; p. 64, 100, 112.
Zola (Émile), « Le Paradis des chats », Nouveaux Contes
 à Ninon, 1874 ; p. 130.

IN THE SAME COLLECTION IN FRENCH

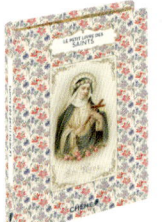
Le petit livre des saints

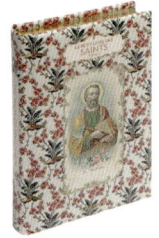
Le petit livre des saints II

Le petit livre des anges

Le petit livre de la Bible

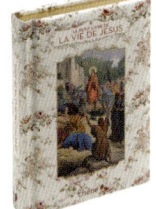
Le petit livre de la vie de Jésus

Le petit livre de Marie

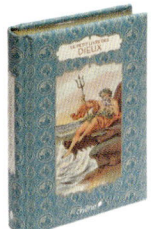
Le petit livre des dieux

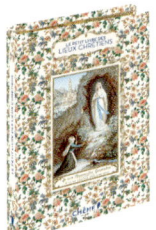
Le petit livre des lieux chrétiens

Le petit livre de Noël

IN THE SAME COLLECTION IN FRENCH

Le petit livre des rois de France

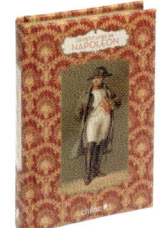

Le petit livre de Napoléon

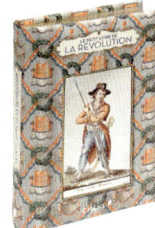

Le petit livre de la Révolution

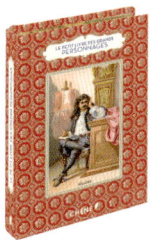

Le petit livre des grands personnages

Le petit livre des citations historiques

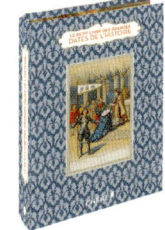

Le petit livre des grandes dates de l'histoire

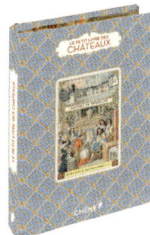

Le petit livre des châteaux

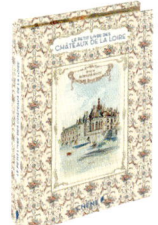

Le petit livre des châteaux de la Loire

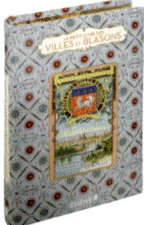

Le petit livre des villes et blasons

IN THE SAME COLLECTION IN FRENCH

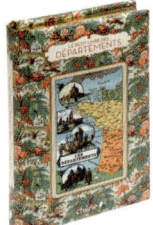

Le petit livre
des départements

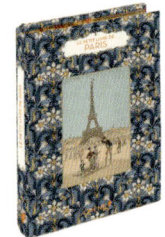

Le petit livre
de Paris

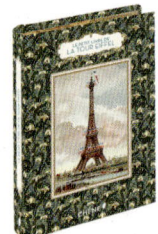

Le petit livre
de la tour Eiffel

Le petit livre
de la Bretagne

Le petit livre
de la France
gourmande

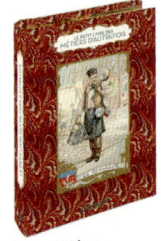

Le petit livre
des métiers d'autrefois

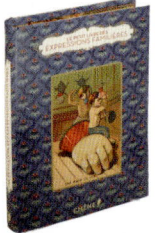

Le petit livre des
expressions familières

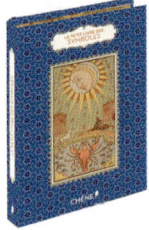

Le petit livre
des symboles

Le petit livre
des jeux d'enfants

IN THE SAME COLLECTION IN FRENCH

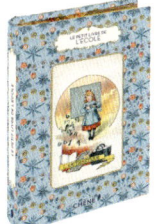

Le petit livre
de l'école

Le petit livre
des fleurs

Le petit livre
des arbres

Le petit livre
des plantes
médicinales

Le petit livre
des champignons

Le petit livre
des chats

Le petit livre
des oiseaux

Le petit livre
du Japon

All images in this book are property of the private collection of Éditions du Chêne. Cover © Collection Kharbine-Tapabor ; Background © iStockphoto.

© 2017 Éditions du Chêne – Hachette Livre for the English edition
© 2015 Éditions du Chêne – Hachette Livre for the original edition
www.editionsduchene.fr

Editorial Director: Flavie Gaidon
with the collaboration of Franck Friès
Editor: Fanny Martin
Artistic Director: Claire Mieyeville
Under the direction of: Sabine Houplain
Proofreading: Myriam Blanc
Translation © Éditions du Chêne – Hachette Livre, 2017
Translation by James Geist

Sales and partnerships: Mathilde Barrois
mbarrois@hachette-livre.fr
Press Relations: Hélène Maurice
hmaurice@hachette-livre.fr
English Layout: Vincent Lanceau
Layout and photoengraving: CGI

Published by Éditions du Chêne
(58 rue Jean Bleuzen, CS 70007, 92178 Vanves Cedex)
Printed in China by Guangzhou Hengyuan Printing
Copyright Registration: september 2017
ISBN : 978-2-81231-740-8
19/5564/7